E PAR
Parker, Victoria.
Slippery or sticky /
Victoria Parker.

Is it...?

slippery or sticky

Vic Parker

Chicago, Illinois

© 2005 Raintree
Published by Raintree, a division of Reed Elsevier, Inc.
Chicago, Illinois
Customer Service 888-363-4266
Visit our website at www.raintreelibrary.com

Color Reproduction by Dot Gradations Ltd, UK.
Printed and bound in China by South China Printing Company.
09 08 07 06 05
10 9 8 7 6 5 4 3 2 1

Library of Congress Cataloging-in-Publication Data:
Parker, Victoria.
 Slippery or sticky / Victoria Parker.
     p. cm. — (Is it?)
 Includes index.
 ISBN 1-4109-0767-8 (lib. bdg.) — ISBN 1-4109-0772-4 (pbk.)
 1. Touch—Juvenile literature. 2. Matter—Properties—Juvenile literature. [1. Touch. 2. Matter—Properties.
3. Show-and-tell presentations.] I. Title. II. Series: Parker, Victoria. Is it?
 QP451.P375 2004
 612.8'8—dc22

                                    2003021649

Acknowledgments
The publishers would like to thank Gareth Boden for permission to reproduce photographs.

Cover photograph reproduced with permission of Gareth Boden.

Every effort has been made to contact copyright holders of any material reproduced in this book.
Any omissions will be rectified in subsequent printings if notice is given to the publishers.

Some words are shown in bold, **like this**. You can find out what they mean by looking at the glossary on page 24.

Contents

A Treasure Hunt 4

Search for Something Slippery 6

Snack on Something Sticky 8

Slippery and Sloppy 10

Outside 12

In the Sun 14

Inside 16

Sticky Surprise 18

Slippery and Sticky 20

At School 22

Glossary 24

Index 24

A Treasure Hunt

At school, we are learning about slippery and sticky things.

We will bring in things from home.

Search for Something Slippery

Water makes this bar of soap slippery.

We will put the soap
in the basket.

Snack on Something Sticky

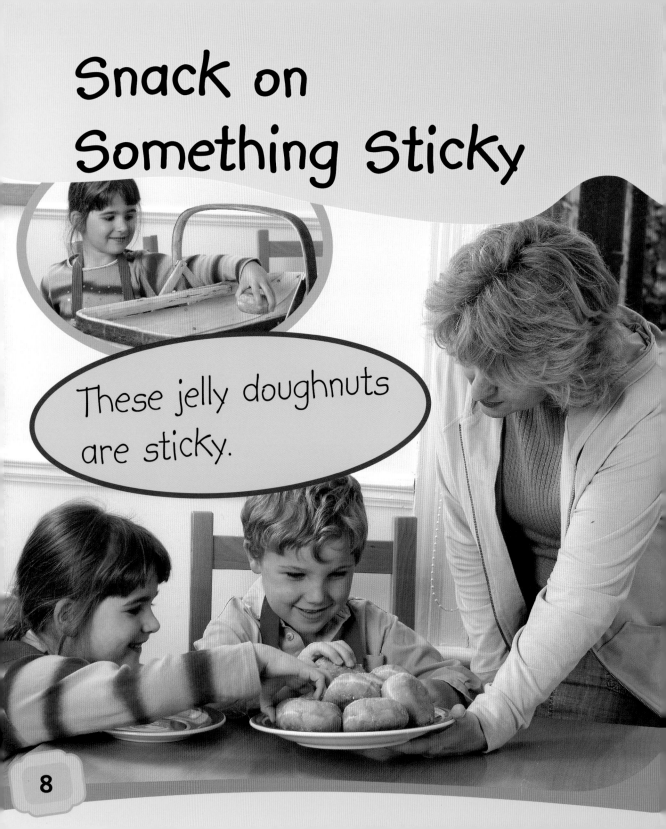

These jelly doughnuts are sticky.

We will take
one to school.

9

Slippery and Sloppy

These beans are slippery.

They are too sloppy for school!

Our plastic aprons
are slippery.

We can take
those to school.

11

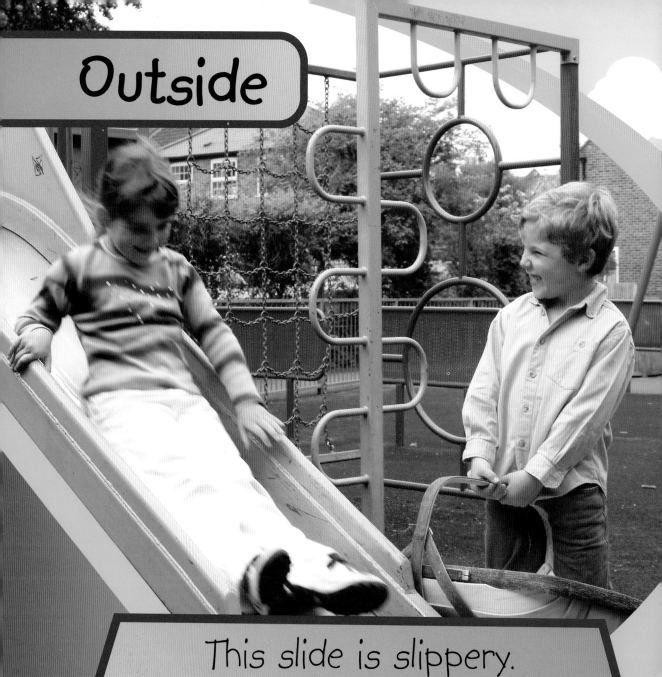

This slide is slippery.
It is too big for the basket.

The **buds** on this plant are sticky.

We can take those to school.

In the Sun

Sunscreen is slippery.

Ice pops are slippery and sticky!

15

Inside

Polish makes the floor slippery.

Whoops!

A sticky bandage will make your knee feel better.

Sticky Surprise

Sticky tape can help us wrap this present.

We can take some to school.

The backs of these stickers are sticky, too.

Slippery and Sticky

This hair **gel** is slippery in the jar.

It makes sticky spikes on my head!

21

At School

sticky things

22

Here is our collection of slippery and sticky things.

slippery things

Glossary

bud part of a plant that can turn into a flower

gel clear, shiny substance used on hair

polish special paste used to clean and shine floors

sunscreen lotion or cream that can protect skin from the sun's rays

Index

apron 11

bandage 17

beans 10

bud 13

collection 23

doughnut 8–9

hair gel 20–21

home 5

ice pop 15

plant 13

polish 16

school . . . 4, 9, 10, 11, 13, 18, 22

slide 12

soap 6–7

sticker 19

sunscreen 14

tape 18